"Resources made by and for people of color who are looking to grow in contemplative Christian practices are few and far between, but Made for PAX is an oasis in a spiritual desert. Their commitment to empowering and raising up voices as part of the global majority is a testament to their shalom-filled activism. The Made for PAX Bible Study Series is a thoughtful resource for folks who are passionate about fostering the flourishing of all."
Jenai Auman, writer and author of *Othered*

"We long for integrity—in ourselves, in society, in the church. I love how the Made for PAX Bible Study Series embodies integrity in both what they present and how they present it. Addressing important topics often neglected by the church, these books call us to live out a holistic faith—and do so by engaging us holistically as readers. Here are pages filled with poems, prayers, visual art, embodied practices, and more, inviting us to join Jesus, step by step, breath by breath, in the work of cultivating integrity and shalom in ourselves and in the world."
Michael Stalcup, poet

"The Made for PAX Bible Study Series is a gift for anyone seeking contemplative scriptural learning. These well-structured studies offer engaging writing and thoughtfully chosen topics. The units on mental health and migration are particularly timely and important, addressing crucial contemporary issues. This is a valuable resource for those seeking deeper understanding, centering often decentered voices."
Guesnerth Josué Perea, director of Black Lives and Contemplation and the Center for Spiritual Imagination

"*Let Peace Reign* is the study guide we need for this moment. Through reflection questions, grounding practices, and Scripture discussions, Drew Jackson curates multiple pathways for participants to engage in authentic peacemaking, rooted in the gospel of shalom that justly restores right relationships in communities and systems. I wholeheartedly recommend this contemplative resource to every follower of Christ called and committed to healing and restoring the brokenness around us. *Let Peace Reign* provides a faithful, practical roadmap for this transformative work of justice and peace."
José Humphreys III, author of *Seeing Jesus in East Harlem* and *Ecosystems of Jubilee*

"*Let Peace Reign* is the resource the church needs right now! It is a justice-rooted guide calling God's people to embody the peacemaking of Jesus. This isn't philosophical abstractions about shalom; as you work through the pages, you are prepared to live it out in a wounded world."
Drew G. I. Hart, associate professor of theology at Messiah University and author of *Making It Plain: Why We Need Anabaptism and the Black Church*

"Drew Jackson calls us to a faith that refuses complacency, showing how the arc of Scripture bends toward justice and peace. *Let Peace Reign* is a prophetic guide to rebuilding a just world where all can flourish, embodying Jesus' radical love to transform our communities and lives."
Sandra María Van Opstal, pastor, author, and executive director of Chasing Justice

LET PEACE REIGN

Love, Justice, and Dignity in God's Kingdom

A 6-WEEK INTERACTIVE BIBLE STUDY

DREW JACKSON

An imprint of InterVarsity Press
Downers Grove, Illinois

InterVarsity Press
P.O. Box 1400 | Downers Grove, IL 60515-1426
ivpress.com | email@ivpress.com

Written by Drew Jackson

InterVarsity Press® is the publishing division of InterVarsity Christian Fellowship/USA®. For more information, visit intervarsity.org.

While any stories in this book are true, some names and identifying information may have been changed to protect the privacy of individuals.

Published in association with Joy Eggerichs Reed of Punchline Agency.

The publisher cannot verify the accuracy or functionality of website URLs used in this book beyond the date of publication.

Cover design: Faceout Studio, Tim Green
Interior design: Nat Maxey
Cover image: © aleksandarvelasevic / DigitalVision Vectors via Getty Images
Interior images: Made for PAX

ISBN 978-1-5140-1298-7 (print)
ISBN 978-1-5140-1299-4 (digital)

Printed in Colombia ♾

Library of Congress Cataloging-in-Publication Data
A catalog record for this book is available from the Library of Congress.

30 29 28 27 26 25 | 8 7 6 5 4 3 2 1

CONTENTS

Let Peace Reign

With PEACE

—

Do you believe the world can be changed?

Your relationships mended?
Your past addressed?
Your future improved?
Our churches active?

Our land healed?
Our bodies protected?
Our politics reformed?

With PEACE, this is possible.

With the Peace of Jesus—
All things are being made new.

With Peace, a better world is nearing.

Welcome

Welcome to this six-week study on peace and justice!

This study invites you into the story of God in order to see how just living and peacemaking are central to Christian discipleship. By the time you complete all six sessions, you will (1) gain a biblical foundation for peace, justice, and the gospel; (2) understand how the story of peace impacts your whole life as a follower of Jesus; and (3) know how to bring the peacemaking and justice of Jesus into your neighborhood, your workplace, your activism, your family, and your friendships.

Most importantly, this study offers hope. In the midst of a world torn apart by racial injustice, trauma, and pain, God is offering you a better way. This study is an invitation into the peace of Jesus, which transforms the world with all the very good things God has for creation.

How to Use this Study

Here is a bird's-eye view of our six-week study.

Session One	The Story of Peace	We are brought into the story of God to help bring about peace and justice for all.
Session Two	The Establishment of Peace	God established a world flowing with peace and justice.
Session Three	The Disruption of Peace	Humanity disrupts the peace and justice God established.
Session Four	The Call of Peace	The prophets call the people of God to practice peace and justice.
Session Five	The Climax of Peace	Shalom is restored through the person and work of Jesus Christ.
Session Six	The Consummation of Peace	King Jesus returns to renew all things once and for all.

EACH SESSION

01 Session Topic: Presents an overview of the week's topic.

02 Preparation: Provides an opportunity to prepare for the study through prayer and reflection questions.

03 Manifesto—Scripture Reading: Includes a Scripture reading that serves as the Manifesto statement (declaration) for the session.

04 Myth & Material—Seven to Twelve Minute Video: Offers a video that covers the Myth (lies we believe) & Material (central truths) for the session.

05 Small Group Discussion: Prompts small group discussion with questions. Discussion is the central part of this journey where you have the opportunity to allow the Spirit of God to move you in the direction you should go.

06 Motion—Embodied Action: Concludes with a Motion section for you to practice throughout the following week and lead you toward more concrete embodied action.

ENGAGING THIS STUDY

Set aside a designated day and time for a weekly gathering—in person or virtually—for the next six weeks. The Introduction offers foundational thoughts and the opportunity for reflection that will frame the subsequent weeks. The session videos are accessed through the QR codes in the book. These videos were created with a group in mind—that you would watch the video together and then immediately engage in the content that follows. But individuals still have personal access to the videos, in case someone misses a group gathering. At the end of each session, participants are given prompts that encourage reflection on the session's key themes throughout the week.

What If?

What if I told you that the way things are, are not the way they have to be? What if the massive gap between rich and poor didn't have to be the status quo? What if our prisons didn't have to be overpopulated, and our environment didn't have to be overtaxed? What if we didn't have to convince the world that Black lives matter? What if women didn't have to say "me too" anymore? What if that one friendship that you thought would never recover could find new life? What if you could live knowing that you do belong and that you are loved?

If you're doubtful, I'd understand. We live in a world where believing that a different way is possible just seems to get more and more difficult every morning we open our eyes. During the Covid-19 pandemic, I remember reading articles about the increased risks that those in NYC public housing and jails faced. This seems to always be the story—that the threat of death pounds more loudly at the doors of our friends and neighbors relegated to the margins of society.

It should not be this way! It should not be that, as a father of two beautiful Black girls, I have to constantly remind them that the hair on their heads is a crown fit for royalty, and not odd or weird, because Western culture asserts that whiteness is the standard for beauty. A deep longing for something new rises within me when I think about the times I have been stopped by police officers and am immediately met with the question, "Whose car is this?" as if a young Black man could only be driving a nice car if it were stolen.

It should not be this way!

Your experiences may not be the same as mine, but each of us, I'm sure, could share our own stories that have moved us to desperately desire a different world. It seems like our world keeps inventing new ways to be out of sorts. But, even as I say these words, there is something within me—within us—that knows that things were not meant to be this way.

It Comes Down to Relationships

From our deep interior questions about identity to the large systemic concerns about injustice, our world has layers of broken relationships. The first chapter of the book of Genesis contains the biblical story about the origins of the universe, and it's here that we learn that God created the world and everything within it and then declared that all of creation was very good.

The picture of beautiful bonds of love existing within creation is shalom.

The goodness of creation was not primarily about natural things being good in and of themselves. Rather, it's important to understand that the ancient Hebrew concept of goodness was located in the relationships between things. In other words, the very essence of God's creation consisted of very good, beautiful, and strong relationships between God and humanity, between humans themselves, between humanity and the whole of the created order, and between humanity and the systems and structures that govern us. Goodness even existed in our relationship with our own selves. This picture of beautiful bonds of love existing within creation is what the Hebrew writers would later come to refer to as *shalom*, or, as we now say, *peace*.

Shalom is the perfection of God's creation, a state in which all parties are able to flourish in relationship with one another in the fullness of who and what God has made them to be. Shalom is cosmic and multidimensional, meaning that it moves in many different directions. Cosmic shalom means peace with God, peace with ourselves, and peace with others. In other words, we must look up, look in, and look out for peace. As Lisa Sharon Harper says in her book *The Very Good Gospel: How Everything Wrong Can Be Made Right*:

> Shalom is . . . when everyone has enough. It's when families are healed. It's when shame is renounced and inner freedom is laid hold of. It's when human dignity, bestowed by the image of God in all humanity, is cultivated, protected, and served in families, faith communities, and schools through public policy. Shalom is when the capacity to lead is recognized in every human being and when nations join together to protect the environment.[1]

God Will Make Things Right

Shalom is what our souls long for. But shalom as longing and shalom as reality seem like worlds apart. And even though this talk of shalom might seem at times like a fantasy dreamworld that will always remain outside of our grasp, there is good news. The story that the Bible tells is that we have a God who responds to our deepest longings for things to be made right.

When the Hebrew people were enslaved for centuries in Egypt, God said to Moses in Exodus 3:7-8, "I have observed the misery of my people who are in Egypt; I have heard their cry on account of their taskmasters. Indeed, I know their sufferings, and I have come down to deliver them.'" This same God, who hears our cries and knows our sufferings, has come down once and for all, in the person of Jesus Christ, in order to deliver us by bridging the gap between our soul's longing for shalom and the reality of shalom. Jesus said of himself in Luke 4:18-19: "The Spirit of the Lord is upon me, because he has anointed me to bring good news to the poor. He has sent me to proclaim release to the captives and recovery of sight to the blind, to set free those who are oppressed, to proclaim the year of the Lord's favor." This is the work of shalom in plain terms, and this is why Jesus came.

In the first chapter of his letter to the Colossians, the apostle Paul says that through Christ "God was pleased to reconcile to himself all things, whether on earth or in heaven, by making peace through the blood of his cross" (Colossians 1:20). To reconcile something means to restore what has been broken, to mend what has fallen apart. We know that, in Genesis, God's creation was all about very good relationships. Everything in the universe exists in relationship with everything else—from protons, neutrons, and electrons, all the way out to stars, planets, and galaxies. If one small thing were to get knocked out of orbit, it would have an effect on the whole cosmos.

Shalom is why Jesus came.

The biblical story is that we, as human beings, have been knocked out of orbit. Through our own disobedience and our failure to live out our true vocation as image-bearers of God, we have stepped out of right relationship with God. And this set in motion the disintegration of all the very good relationships that God initially set in place at creation. In putting on flesh in the person of Jesus and stepping into our world that has been knocked out of orbit, God's sole mission was reconciliation. The good news of the gospel is that, in Jesus, God is at work putting back together that which has fallen apart. And the first relationship that God set out to restore is the relationship between God and humanity.

It Starts with Us

The first word that the Bible speaks about humanity is that we are created in the image of God. What that means, in part, is that we were created to reflect the wise rule and council of God into the rest of creation. As image-bearers of God, we were given the responsibility of making sure that all of the very good relationships in God's creation remain very good. We were never meant to exercise authority according to our own wisdom; we were meant to reflect God's wisdom. This is where we went off track. When we dropped the ball, Jesus stepped in to pick it back up again for all of humanity. Through his incarnation, life, death, resurrection, and ascension, Jesus, who the Bible says is the wisdom of God, showed us how to be fully human and paved the way for us to be restored back to right relationship with God.

The glory of God is a human being fully alive.

Now, if humanity can be reconciled to God, find peace with God, and begin, once again, to fully reflect God's wise rule and council, then the whole of creation will breathe a sigh of relief. This is what the apostle Paul means in Romans 8:19 when he says, "the creation waits with eager longing for the revealing of the children of God." In other words, the whole creation is longing for you and me to be our truest selves, awakened to our true humanity, living out our true vocation. And the good news is that Jesus has made this possible! Jesus has both given us access back into the life of God, and has shown us what it looks like to be fully human. As the church father St. Irenaeus famously said, "The glory of God is a human being fully alive." When we say yes to following Jesus, we are saying yes to the call to be fully human. We are saying yes to living out of our deepest identity as children of God. And as Jesus says in Matthew 5:9, children of God do the work of making shalom. We have the beautiful privilege of joining Jesus in the work of peace—the work of co-laboring with Jesus to make all things new.

So, when I say that things don't have to be this way, I mean that there is another way to be human. There is a way of being human that seeks to empower those in poverty, instead of ignoring and continuing to silence their voices. There is a way of being human that labors to see restorative justice instead of retributive justice in our systems of incarceration. There is a way of being human that maintains the dignity of black and brown lives, honors the voices and bodies of women, and cares for our environment. There is a way of being human that puts into practice the cross-shaped art of forgiveness in our relationships. There is a way of being human where we can feel that we belong and where we can know that we are loved. The first step in this journey of discovering peace within ourselves and laboring for peace with others is to find peace with God in whose image we are created. This is the way of shalom. This is the way of peace. This is the way of Jesus.

REFLECTION QUESTIONS

01 Why have you shown up for this journey?

02 What makes you want to learn more about peace and justice?

03 How do you define *peace*? How do you define *justice*?

SESSION ONE

The Story of Peace

The St
Peace

Establishment
Disruption
Call
Climax
Consummation

ory of

This week is about a story.
It is about the story of all stories.
In this story, you will find your place.

We begin Session One with an exploration of the concepts of peace and justice within the story of God. Whether you're passionate about justice, eager to learn how to become a peacemaker, or unsure about how justice and the gospel coincide, we're glad you're here. We recognize that some of you have been journeying as peacemakers and justice seekers for quite some time, while others might be exploring these concepts for the first time. That's okay. Wherever you're at right now, take a moment to prepare your body and heart for engagement with this week's session. If you're doing this as a group study, come with a posture of humility and openness to other people's perspectives.

Pulse Check

Share some of your answers from the introduction's reflection questions.

01 Why have you shown up for this journey?

02 What makes you want to learn more about peace and justice?

03 How do you define *peace*? How do you define *justice*?

Preparation

To prepare for Session One, follow the grounding practice and read the accompanying prayer. Be present with those you are with, and be attentive to what God might impress on you during this time.

We start with a grounding practice because the world we live in is always on the go. We're often expected to show up, produce, and execute. This is a time for us to come together and consider shalom—God's dream for us to be whole, flourishing, and at peace. Shalom is God's dream for us to be fully human. This grounding practice reminds you to slow down, breathe, and invite the God of Peace to settle you before you begin with the group study.

GROUNDING PRACTICE

Take three Deep Breaths

Inhale: God of Peace
Exhale: I am Here

Inhale: God of Peace
Exhale: I am Yours

Inhale: God of Peace
Exhale: I am Ready

Poem by Drew Jackson

MADE FOR PEACE

It starts with a Word. A very good Word spoken by Creator. Goodness within and goodness between, binding us together, all things tethered by Love.

Shalom.

But then there's a breaking, a fracture within this cosmic bond, knocking protons and electrons out of orbit. No longer moving in unity, but now existing with great autonomy.

Shattered.

We've been lost. Unbound from our identity, searching for our vocation, working to locate ourselves within this great wide world.

Seeking.

But then comes the in-breaking. The very good Word made flesh and bone, sought us out and made this shattered world home, all to bring us back to the beginning—back to shalom.

Slaughtered.

Because we resist with tight fists, holding onto our way. But Life cannot be held within tombs and in graves. Once again, fresh breath was blown into this clay.

Sent.

To rebind and restore. With new vision for this mission we were created for. Fully reflecting this imprinted Image, as we work to bring pax back to existence.

Peace.

Manifesto

Shalom is the perfection of God's creation, a state in which all parties are able to flourish in relationship to one another in the fullness of who and what God has made them.

Colossians 1:15-20

He is the image of the invisible God, the firstborn of all creation, for in him all things in heaven and on earth were created, things visible and invisible, whether thrones or dominions or rulers or powers—all things have been created through him and for him. He himself is before all things, and in him all things hold together. He is the head of the body, the church; he is the beginning, the firstborn from the dead, so that he might come to have first place in everything. For in him all the fullness of God was pleased to dwell, and through him God was pleased to reconcile to himself all things, whether on earth or in heaven, by making peace through the blood of his cross.

God is the author of peace, and peace is essential to life. Peace is inherently relational as peace and justice cannot be known in isolation, and God has invited us to co-labor with him in this pursuit. As God restores our dignity and sets right the relationship between us and God, we in turn reflect the image of God in the world by restoring peace within ourselves and our communities, between us and the systems and structures that govern, and between us and all of creation.

Scan the QR code to watch the Session One Myth & Material video. As you watch the video, write down any statements that stand out to you or thoughts that you have.

Myth

Peace is achieved through oppression and suppression.

Material

Jesus calls us to be peacemakers.

DISCUSSION QUESTIONS

01 In what ways does our world oppress, suppress, and overpower to achieve its version of peace?

02 What is the difference between the peace of this world and the peace of Jesus?

03 What would a more just and peace-filled world look like? How might God be calling you to work with him to make peace in this world?

Benediction

May the Spirit of God bless you with insight and revelation as you take this journey toward peace.

May you be led by Jesus to glimpse a new world where love is the language we speak and shalom binds us together.

May you be filled with a holy expectation that will not rest content until you encounter the living God.

And may you awaken to the reality that you are a child of God created to make peace in the midst of a desperate world.

Amen.

Go in Peace.

Motion

Centering Down Meditation

_ a guide by spiritual director
Osheta Moore

There are many pictures of peacemaking and peacemakers that we have to contend with. To some, peacemakers are gentle, kind, and passive people who resist conflict at all costs. To others, peacemakers are brave and selfless people who do things like offer themselves as human shields in war-torn countries or spend years studying diplomacy or peacemaking. When we do not have a picture of peacemakers and peacemaking that includes us—just as we are in our regular lives—then Jesus' Beatitude teaching on peacemaking feels tone-deaf and unrealistic. Shalom, however, is God's invitation to flourishing and wholeness, and from that overflow we create peace in the world around us.

Throughout this upcoming week, we're going to meditate on a reflection from Howard Thurman. Thurman was a major influence on Dr. Martin Luther King Jr. It is said Dr. King carried the Bible and a copy of Thurman's *Jesus and the Disinherited* constantly because Thurman's commitment to holistic activism—one that engages body, mind, soul, spirit, and nonviolence—was essential to the civil rights movement.

Centering down is a contemplative practice that asks you to clear your mind of all the distractions that prevent you from sensing God's closeness and the Spirit's encouragement.

HOW TO MEDITATE WITH THE PASSAGE

Read the reflection from Howard Thurman.

Ask yourself: "What is keeping me from feeling centered?" Spend five minutes in silence.

What pictures come to your mind when you think of centering down? Read the passage again, this time imagining yourself as centered.

This week, journal or ponder the questions Thurman asks.

How Good to Center Down!

Howard Thurman

How good it is to center down!
To sit quietly and see one's self pass by!
The streets of our minds seethe with endless traffic;
Our spirits resound with clashing, with noisy silences,
While something deep within hungers and thirsts for the still moment and the resting lull.
With full intensity we seek, ere thicket passes, a fresh sense of order in our living;
A direction, a strong sure purpose that will structure our confusion and bring meaning in our chaos.
We look at ourselves in this waiting moment—the kinds of people we are.
The questions persist: what are we doing with our lives?—what are the motives that order our days?
What is the end of our doings? Where are we trying to go?
Where do we put the emphasis and where are our values focused?
For what end do we make sacrifices? Where is my treasure and what do I love most in life?
What do I hate most in life and to what am I true?
Over and over the questions beat upon the waiting moment.
As we listen, floating up through all of the jangling echoes of our turbulence, there is a sound of another kind—
A deeper note which only the stillness of the heart makes clear.
It moves directly to the core of our being. Our questions are answered,
Our spirits refreshed, and we move back into the traffic of our daily round
With the peace of the Eternal in our step.
How good it is to center down![1]

SESSION TWO

The Establishment of Peace

The Est
ment o

—

Establishment

Disruption

Call

Climax

Consummation

ablish-
f Peace

This week is about beginnings.
It is about how the world was made.
It is about the Establishment of Peace.

Last week set the stage for God's vision of peace in the world. In Session Two, we will learn why and how God established peace. We hope you are able to see the world God created and help envision a world where God's flourishing, peace, justice, and love are possible for the entire created order.

Pulse Check

Last week you learned about God's dream for shalom and meditated on Howard Thurman's reflection "How Good to Center Down!" Spend some time sharing how you felt about practicing silence and stillness. Was it difficult? Easy? Much needed? Meditation is difficult, especially in this busy world. Celebrate with each other the times you were able to commit to stillness and silence this past week.

Share your answers to one of the questions that Thurman poses in "How Good to Center Down!":

01 What are we doing with our lives? What are the motives that order our days?

02 What is the end of our doings?

03 Where are we trying to go?

04 Where do we put the emphasis and where are our values focused?

05 For what end do we make sacrifices?

06 Where is my treasure and what do I love most in life?

Preparation

To prepare for Session Two, follow the grounding practice and read the accompanying prayer. Be present with those you are with, and be attentive to what God might impress on you during this time.

We start with a grounding practice because the world we live in is always on the go. We're often expected to show up, produce, and execute. This is a time for us to come together and consider shalom—God's dream for us to be whole, flourishing, and at peace. Shalom is God's dream for us to be fully human. This grounding practice reminds you to slow down, breathe, and invite the God of Peace to settle you before you begin with the group study.

GROUNDING PRACTICE

Take three Deep Breaths

Inhale: God of Peace
Exhale: I am Here

Inhale: God of Peace
Exhale: I am Yours

Inhale: God of Peace
Exhale: I am Ready

Prayer

God of all power—
Whose presence is not bound,
Whose words are not weak,
Whose identity cannot be owned.
I am Your child but I am unlike You—
My presence feels invisible,
My words feel empty,
My identity is both owned and disowned.

I need Your peace to tell me the truth
About how You can heal a girl with many parts.
Part angry,
Part anxious,
Part antagonistic,
Part Anglo,
Part Asian,
Part 破.[1]
What can You do with the parts of me that feel at war
with the world?[2]

Manifesto

God established a world flowing with peace and justice.

Genesis 1:1-5, 26-28

When God began to create the heavens and the earth, the earth was complete chaos, and darkness covered the face of the deep, while a wind from God swept over the face of the waters. Then God said, "Let there be light," and there was light. And God saw that the light was good, and God separated the light from the darkness. God called the light Day, and the darkness he called Night. And there was evening and there was morning, the first day. . . . Then God said, "Let us make humans in our image, according to our likeness, and let them have dominion over the fish of the sea and over the birds of the air and over the cattle and over all the wild animals of the earth and over every creeping thing that creeps upon the earth."
So God created humans in his image, in the image of God he created them; male and female he created them.
God blessed them, and God said to them, "Be fruitful and multiply and fill the earth and subdue it and have dominion over the fish of the sea and over the birds of the air and over every living thing that moves upon the earth."

At the beginning of human history, God looks out over creation and says that it is very good (Genesis 1:31). There is a perfect relationship between God and humans. There is a perfect relationship between humans and their surroundings. There is no pain, death, suffering, injustice, or hunger. This fullness of peace and harmony is what justice looks like.

Justice can mean the state of things being right; it can also refer to the process by which things are being straightened out, being set right. In the beginning there was justice because all things were right. All things were in harmony (right relationships) and, in this way, there was shalom. This picture of wholeness and harmony is what the Bible has in view when it speaks about justice. Because justice is all about things being rightly related to each other in fair and equitable ways, justice is required in order for shalom to be a reality.

The first humans are made in God's image. They are called to reflect God's love, justice, and peace in the world. Adam and Eve experience the completeness and the perfect interconnectedness of all of creation. This is the way things are meant to be.

Scan the QR code to watch the Session Two Myth & Material video. As you watch the video, write down any statements that stand out to you or thoughts that you have.

Myth

Our purpose in this world is to achieve our own comfort, security, and happiness.

Material

Jesus calls us to practice self-giving love.

DISCUSSION QUESTIONS

01 Think about the question *Why am I here?* What images, thoughts, and emotions come to mind?

02 In what ways are you tempted to believe that your life should be about your own comfort, security, and happiness?

03 What is our purpose in this world according to Jesus?

04 What might it look like for you to practice self-giving love within your sphere of influence this week?

Benediction

May the peace of the Lord Jesus Christ
go with you wherever he may send you.

May the Spirit ground you in the truth
that you were created with divine purpose.

May you take up your God-given vocation
to be a peacemaker with courage and tenacity.

And may you be overwhelmed with the love
of our triune God in whose image you are made.

Amen.

Go in Peace.

Motion

Journal to Find Shalom

_ a guide by spiritual director Osheta Moore

Educator and author Parker Palmer said, "Before I can tell my life what I want to do with it, I must listen to my life telling me who I am."[3] In this week's motion practice, you will begin discerning your unique spiritual gifts that will allow you to create shalom.

Journal about a time *when you felt you were firing on all cylinders, and you felt like you were not only doing what you are good at but what you love.* Then consider what will help you know how God is inviting you to be a peacemaker in your context. For example, if money were not an issue and you had all the time in the world, what one brokenness would you address and how would you do it? What is a dream that makes you feel alive?

For me, I want to own a large farm with lots of animals with many rooms, where teen girls of color who find themselves in unexpected pregnancies could come. They could be cared for during their pregnancies, and use their time on the farm to heal and receive vision for their futures with their children.

From this dream I've invested in nonprofits that offer holistic care to pregnant teens; I've mentored pregnant teens; and I was on the board of a transition home for teens. This is one area God has called me to create shalom in small, intentional ways.

Share your journal entry with a trusted spiritual mentor or friend this week.

SESSION THREE

The Disruption of Peace

The Di
tion of

—

Establishment
Disruption
Call
Climax
Consummation

srup-
Peace

This week is about how things went wrong.
This week is about how creation was corrupted.
It is about the Disruption of Peace.

Last week we learned how God established peace and justice in the garden of Eden. This perfect combination of peace and justice is known as shalom. Session Three explores how peace was disrupted. We all know too well how the world is broken, how our bodies are broken, how creation is hurting, and how we struggle to cope with the brokenness we see around us. We will be pressing into "what went wrong" in order to begin imagining how things can be "set right."

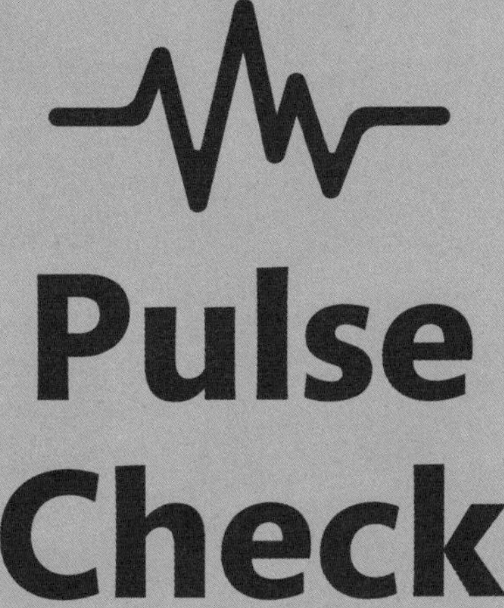

Pulse Check

Share with each other your dream of shalom from Session Two's Motion exercise.

01 If money were not an issue and you had all the time in the world, what one brokenness would you address and how would you do it? If you feel comfortable, pray for each other's shalom dreams.

Preparation

To prepare for Session Three, follow the grounding practice and read the accompanying prayer. Be present with those you are with, and be attentive to what God might impress on you during this time.

We start with a grounding practice because the world we live in is always on the go. We're often expected to show up, produce, and execute. This is a time for us to come together and consider shalom—God's dream for us to be whole, flourishing, and at peace. Shalom is God's dream for us to be fully human. This grounding practice reminds you to slow down, breathe, and invite the God of Peace to settle you before you begin with the group study.

GROUNDING PRACTICE

Take three Deep Breaths

Inhale: God of Peace
Exhale: I am Here

Inhale: God of Peace
Exhale: I am Yours

Inhale: God of Peace
Exhale: I am Ready

Prayer

"All who hate me whisper together about me;
they imagine the worst for me."
(Psalm 41:7)

O God,

My soul's been abused by sin—mine and theirs. Bitterness took root like wormwood, and though I've confessed it, the shame lingers.

It whispers in my heart,
"You won't recover."
"You're a fraud."
"You're hopeless."

My own heart plays the enemy, imagining the worst for me. When I would come to you, I shy away. What if all my "coming" is just fake?

O Lord, bring shalom to my broken soul. Please make my feeble attempts to come to you mean something.[1]

Manifesto

Humanity disrupts the peace and justice God established.

Genesis 3:8-21

They heard the sound of the LORD God walking in the garden at the time of the evening breeze, and the man and his wife hid themselves from the presence of the LORD God among the trees of the garden. But the LORD God called to the man and said to him, "Where are you?" He said, "I heard the sound of you in the garden, and I was afraid, because I was naked, and I hid myself." He said, "Who told you that you were naked? Have you eaten from the tree of which I commanded you not to eat?" The man said, "The woman whom you gave to be with me, she gave me fruit from the tree, and I ate." Then the LORD God said to the woman, "What is this that you have done?" The woman said, "The serpent tricked me, and I ate." The LORD God said to the serpent,

"Because you have done this,
cursed are you among all animals
and among all wild creatures;
upon your belly you shall go,
and dust you shall eat
all the days of your life.
I will put enmity between you and the woman
and between your offspring and hers;
he will strike your head,
and you will strike his heel."
To the woman he said,
"I will make your pangs in childbirth exceedingly great;
in pain you shall bring forth children,
yet your desire shall be for your husband,
and he shall rule over you."
And to the man he said,
"Because you have listened to the voice of your wife
and have eaten of the tree
about which I commanded you,
'You shall not eat of it,'
cursed is the ground because of you;
in toil you shall eat of it all the days of your life;
thorns and thistles it shall bring forth for you;

and you shall eat the plants of the field.
By the sweat of your face
you shall eat bread
until you return to the ground,
for out of it you were taken;
you are dust,
and to dust you shall return."
The man named his wife Eve because she was the mother of all living. And the LORD God made garments of skins for the man and for his wife and clothed them.

Early on in human history, as the book of Genesis outlines, Adam and Eve decide to act outside of their design. They disobey God, feel shame for the first time, and hide themselves from God (Genesis 3:8). The perfect peace that God established was disrupted because of sin. And, as Paul summarizes, sin leads to death (Romans 5:12; 6:23), which is the opposite of peace.

As the story of human history unfolds, we see a disruption in the relationship between God and humans (Genesis 3:17-19); between people (Genesis 3:15); and between humans and the rest of creation. We also see a severing of relationships with our own bodies, our very selves (Genesis 3:14-19). This is what injustice looks like. It is when there is no harmony, no peace. The life that God intended for the created order devolves into death and decay (Genesis 3:19). These are the results of sin (i.e., living outside of our original design).

However, from the book of Genesis onward, God initiates a plan of renewal and rescue. This is the process of bringing justice, of making everything right again, of restoring peace. The plan of rescue is initiated through a man named Abraham, through whom God promises that all nations will be blessed (Genesis 12:1-3; 18:18). How will this happen? God says that he has "chosen [Abraham], that he may charge his children and his household after him to keep the way of the LORD by doing righteousness and justice, so that the LORD may bring about for Abraham what he has promised him" (Genesis 18:19).

God's people, Abraham's descendants, the people of Israel, embark on a journey that includes slavery, liberation, wandering in the wilderness, inheritance of the Promised Land, adopting a system of kings, and eventual exile. All along the way, God provides glimpses of peace, and God also promises to fully restore the peace that was lost in the garden.

Scan the QR code to watch the Session Three Myth & Material video. As you watch the video, write down any statements that stand out to you or thoughts that you have.

Myth

The way things are, are the way things are.

Material

Jesus came to change our world for the better.

DISCUSSION QUESTIONS

01 How have you experienced the disruption of peace in your life this week (as well as in your life as a whole)?

02 In what ways are you tempted to believe the myth that things are just the way they are?

03 As you look out at the world, in what specific areas does your heart long for change?

Spend some time meditating on your answers from the discussion questions. Write a prayer of confession in the space below.

Benediction

May God bless you with tears of lament
that mourn over the injustice of our world.

May you be blessed with a holy discontent
over the way the world is.

May the Spirit of Jesus shake you out of complacency
and fill you with all manner of hope.

And may you experience the transforming power
of God in your own life, in all the places
where you are desperate for change.

Amen.

Go in Peace.

Motion

Kyrie Eleison / Daily Examen

_ a guide by spiritual director Osheta Moore

The *Kyrie* translates into English as follows:
Kyrie eleison: Lord, have mercy
Christe eleison: Christ, have mercy
Kyrie eleison: Lord, have mercy

This ritual song dates from early Greek (Eastern) Christian liturgies and has retained its Greek text in the Latin (Western) rite. In the Eastern tradition, the Kyrie is still used as a response in litanies. By the end of the eighth century in the Roman (Western) church, the Kyrie was used as a separate song, often in a nine-fold form: a three-time repetition of its three lines, in which the priest utters the first line, the congregation or (more likely) a choir responds with the second, and the priest responds with the third. The Kyrie became part of the Ordinary (the unvarying parts) of the Roman Catholic Mass, chanted at the very beginning of the service.

Some liturgies of the Reformation continued to use the Kyrie in connection with confession of sin or with the reading of the Ten Commandments. Like other ancient biblical and liturgical expressions (such as *amen, alleluia, hosanna, maranatha*), the Kyrie is a prayer that ties us to Christians from all times and places.

Find a rendition of the Gregorian chant "Kyrie Eleison" on your favorite music app or YouTube this week and listen to it twice a day: once in the morning and then again in the evening.

After you listen to it in the evening, consider practicing the Daily Examen (provided below). The Daily Examen is an ancient Ignatian practice of reflecting on your day and looking for ways you've connected with God's presence, as well as opportunities you missed to create peace.

FIVE STEPS OF REFLECTION

01 Ask God to give you light: "Open my eyes to your presence throughout my day. Let me see this day from your perspective."

02 Give thanks to God for the gift of the day and the gift of the time to reflect.

03 Review the day. Invite the Holy Spirit to show you key moments through your day. Pay attention to your body's response. Pay attention to "If only . . ." or "I wish I . . ." thoughts. This is the Spirit illuminating your heart's desire for shalom and maybe an opportunity you missed.

04 Face these shortcomings in the light of Jesus' love. Imagine the Lord examining your missed opportunity with love and patience on his face, not judgment and anger. Confess your missed opportunity and allow the Lord to offer forgiveness with this one line: "Go, and sin no more."

05 End the time by owning your belovedness. Say, "I am beloved." How does this reality inspire you to seek peace tomorrow in a way that allows another person to own their belovedness?

SESSION FOUR

The Call of Peace

The Ca
Peace

Establishment

Disruption

Call

Climax

Consummation

ll of

This week is about working toward peace and justice. This week is about God's call to fight for what is right. It is about the Call of Peace in our lives.

In the previous sessions we learned about the establishment of peace and the disruption of peace. We learned how the disruption of peace leads to sin, death, and a brokenness that affects so many parts of our world. In Session Four, we will talk about the call of peace. Through the darkness of a broken world, a prophetic witness begins to emerge in Israel. God begins calling the prophets, the teachers, and the people to restore peace in the world. What will this restoration look like? What does restoration mean? Who is restoration for? This week, we will discover how we might reimagine a better world.

Pulse Check

Share with your group if you practiced the Examen throughout the week. If so, which step was the hardest for you?

Preparation

To prepare for Session Four, follow the grounding practice and read the accompanying prayer. Be present with those you are with, and be attentive to what God might impress on you during this time.

We start with a grounding practice because the world we live in is always on the go. We're often expected to show up, produce, and execute. This is a time for us to come together and consider shalom—God's dream for us to be whole, flourishing, and at peace. Shalom is God's dream for us to be fully human. This grounding practice reminds you to slow down, breathe, and invite the God of Peace to settle you before you begin with the group study.

GROUNDING PRACTICE

Take three Deep Breaths

Inhale: God of Peace
Exhale: I am Here

Inhale: God of Peace
Exhale: I am Yours

Inhale: God of Peace
Exhale: I am Ready

Prayer

Father,
I come with balled fists,
Clenched in frustration, anger, pain.
I need your shalom.

Father,
I come with a tight grip,
Grasping things that I want to keep.
Give me your shalom.

Father,
I come with curled fingers,
Tense with worry and fear.
Remind me of your shalom.

Father,
See my clasped hands.
I don't even want to be here.
The last thing I want to do is pray.
But I remember:
You have covered me with your shalom.

Transform my broken hands into
Open
Surrendered
Lifted
Praising hands
That live in your shalom.[1]

Manifesto

The prophets call the people of God to practice peace and justice.

Amos 5:21-24

I hate, I despise your festivals,
and I take no delight in your solemn assemblies.
Even though you offer me your burnt offerings and grain offerings,
I will not accept them,
and the offerings of well-being of your fatted animals
I will not look upon.
Take away from me the noise of your songs;
I will not listen to the melody of your harps.
But let justice roll down like water
and righteousness like an ever-flowing stream.

Jeremiah 22:15-16

Are you a king
because you compete in cedar?
Did not your father eat and drink
and do justice and righteousness?
Then it was well with him.
He judged the cause of the poor and needy;
then it was well.
Is not this to know me?
says the LORD.

Throughout Israel's difficult history, the prophets make it clear that the people of God are supposed to engage in the godly work of restoring justice in our broken world. Isaiah says justice and righteousness are the only "fruit" God wants from his people, whom he likens to a vineyard (Isaiah 5:7). Similarly, Amos says God is not pleased with empty displays of religion but only desires his people to "let justice roll down like water and righteousness like an ever-flowing stream" (Amos 5:24).

The prophet Jeremiah declares that anyone who claims to have a personal relationship with God will "do justice and righteousness" and plead "the cause of the poor and needy" (Jeremiah 22:15-16). "Is not this to know me? says the LORD" (Jeremiah 22:16). Through Jeremiah God also says to "let those who boast in this, that they understand and know me, that I am the LORD; I act with steadfast love, justice, and righteousness in the earth, for in these things I delight" (Jeremiah 9:24).

Though injustice is everywhere, the prophets are confident there will come a time when justice and peace will be restored (Isaiah 2:2-4; Micah 4:1-3). Isaiah says this will come through a special anointed person, a new David, who will restore everything to the peaceful harmony of all creatures that was present in the beginning (Isaiah 11:1-9; 65:25). Micah says this person from the Davidic tribe of Judah and city of Bethlehem "shall be the one of peace" (Micah 5:5) and Isaiah calls him "Prince of Peace" (Isaiah 9:6). In the meantime, the people of God are to be about the work of restorative justice, enacting glimpses of the fullness of peace as they bear the fruit of justice and righteousness.

Scan the QR code to watch the Session Four Myth & Material video. As you watch the video, write down any statements that stand out to you or thoughts that you have.

Myth

If you speak out against injustice, then you are standing in the way of the unity that God desires.

Material

God requires all of humanity to do justice, love mercy, and walk humbly with our God.

DISCUSSION QUESTIONS

01 What would it look like to do justice, love mercy, and walk humbly with God in your own life?

02 What are some ways that you have seen yourself draw back from the call to do justice?

03 How can you center the practice of justice within your faith? Write down a few practical ideas.

Benediction

May God fill your bones, like the prophet Jeremiah, with the holy fire of justice.

May the Spirit that overtook Amos overtake you and move you to raise your voice until justice rolls down like water and righteousness like a mighty stream.

May you be blessed with vision, like Isaiah, that is able to see God's new world and bear witness to that which is to come.

And may you know, with the clarity of Micah, that you have been called to do justice, love mercy, and walk humbly with God.

Amen.

Go in Peace.

Motion

Seek the Shalom of Your City

_ a guide by spiritual director Osheta Moore

Oftentimes when we think of ending injustice, we look at the major problems of the world and feel overwhelmed. We feel like anything we offer is inadequate.

God has a word for us when we feel this way.

Meditate on Jeremiah 29:7: *"But seek the welfare of the city where I have sent you into exile, and pray to the LORD on its behalf, for in its welfare you will find your welfare."*

God is speaking to his people who have been in captivity in Babylon. Imagine how they must have felt: overwhelmed, under-resourced, insecure, bitter, and anxious to leave. God asks them to stay. Put down roots. Care deeply about the context in which they are placed. To seek its flourishing.

Now reflect on this extended passage from Jeremiah 29:4-7:

> *Thus says the LORD of hosts, the God of Israel, to all the exiles whom I have sent into exile from Jerusalem to Babylon: Build houses and live in them; plant gardens and eat what they produce. Take wives and have sons and daughters; take wives for your sons, and give your daughters in marriage, that they may bear sons and daughters; multiply there, and do not decrease. But seek the welfare of the city where I have sent you into exile, and pray to the LORD on its behalf, for in its welfare you will find your welfare.*

There are four major ways God is asking his peacemakers to show up for their cities:

1. *Care for the land*

2. *Care for the people and build healthy relationships*

3. *Care about the politics*

4. *Pray*

This week, do some research and journal about how you can engage in these four ways in your community. For instance, can you join a park cleanup? Can you email a homeless shelter and see what practical things they need to continue serving their guests? Could you email a school counselor and ask if she needs some resources to serve her students better? Who are the public servants in your city and where do they stand on issues? Note their names and then pray for them.

SESSION FIVE

The Climax of Peace

The Cli
of Pea

Establishment
Disruption
Call
Climax
Consummation

max
ce

This week is about the high point of the story.
This week is about God's rescuing work in Jesus.
It is about the Climax of Peace.

Last week we learned about the prophetic call to peace. We explored the ways in which followers of Jesus enter into the legacy of just living and peacemaking. In Session Five, the story of peace now comes to its climax through King Jesus. When you think of all the suffering in the world, all the brokenness, all the pain, all the injustice—where do we find our solution? Who will walk with humanity and restore creation back to its rightful place? What does rescue look like?

Pulse Check

Last week's Motion challenged us to learn about the unique needs of our city or community.

Share your findings with each other.

Preparation

To prepare for Session Five, follow the grounding practice and read the accompanying prayer. Be present with those you are with, and be attentive to what God might impress on you during this time.

We start with a grounding practice because the world we live in is always on the go. We're often expected to show up, produce, and execute. This is a time for us to come together and consider shalom—God's dream for us to be whole, flourishing, and at peace. Shalom is God's dream for us to be fully human. This grounding practice reminds you to slow down, breathe, and invite the God of Peace to settle you before you begin with the group study.

GROUNDING PRACTICE

Take three Deep Breaths

Inhale: God of Peace
Exhale: I am Here

Inhale: God of Peace
Exhale: I am Yours

Inhale: God of Peace
Exhale: I am Ready

Prayer

Jesus, come.
Into my confusion: Am I from here? From there?
Where am I from?
Jesus, come.
Into the guilt: "I can't believe you are forgetting Spanish!"
Jesus, come.
Into the invalidation: I'm the only Latina in this room.

I'm from everywhere and nowhere, forever longing for home.
I've been racing. I trip, fall, and bruise. Ignore it. Keep on racing—the grit of an immigrant.
And then at times, my vision fogs and fear overcomes my soul. I crumble. I despise everything I know.

" . . . [I] created [your] inmost being [mi hija hermosa], [I] knitted [you] together in [your] mother's womb," Jesus tells me.[1]

Open wounds, oh so real.
My King at the cross.
For me. For all of this.
His scars remain and yet He rose.
He's now sitting in His Heavenly throne!
Gloria a Dios![2]

Manifesto

Peace and justice are restored through the person and work of Jesus Christ.

Luke 4:14-30

Then Jesus, in the power of the Spirit, returned to Galilee, and a report about him spread through all the surrounding region. He began to teach in their synagogues and was praised by everyone. When he came to Nazareth, where he had been brought up, he went to the synagogue on the Sabbath day, as was his custom. He stood up to read, and the scroll of the prophet Isaiah was given to him. He unrolled the scroll and found the place where it was written:

"The Spirit of the Lord is upon me,
because he has anointed me
to bring good news to the poor.
He has sent me to proclaim release to the captives
and recovery of sight to the blind,
to set free those who are oppressed,
to proclaim the year of the Lord's favor."

And he rolled up the scroll, gave it back to the attendant, and sat down. The eyes of all in the synagogue were fixed on him. Then he began to say to them, "Today this scripture has been fulfilled in your hearing." All spoke well of him and were amazed at the gracious words that came from his mouth. They said, "Is this not Joseph's son?" He said to them, "Doubtless you will quote to me this proverb, 'Doctor, cure yourself!' And you will say, 'Do here also in your hometown the things that we have heard you did at Capernaum.'" And he said, "Truly I tell you, no prophet is accepted in his hometown. But the truth is, there were many widows in Israel in the time of Elijah, when the heaven was shut up three years and six months and there was a severe famine over all the land, yet Elijah was sent to none of them except to a widow at Zarephath in Sidon. There were also many with a skin disease in Israel in the time of the prophet Elisha, and none of them was cleansed except Naaman the Syrian." When they heard this, all in the synagogue were filled with rage. They got up, drove him out of the town, and led him to the brow of the hill on which their town was built, so that they might hurl him off the cliff. But he passed through the midst of them and went on his way.

Colossians 1:15-20

He is the image of the invisible God, the firstborn of all creation, for in him all things in heaven and on earth were created, things visible and invisible, whether thrones or dominions or rulers or powers—all things have been created through him and for him. He himself is before all things, and in him all things hold together. He is the head of the body, the church; he is the beginning, the firstborn from the dead, so that he might come to have first place in everything. For in him all the fullness of God was pleased to dwell, and through him God was pleased to reconcile to himself all things, whether on earth or in heaven, by making peace through the blood of his cross.

When the New Testament is written, Israel is under the weight of the Roman Empire, oppressed and subjugated in their own land. It is a dark moment in the life of Israel. They have not heard a word from God or God's prophets in four hundred years. God's people are longing for justice, peace, and salvation to be restored. The world is longing for the peace of God. Jesus is born into this world to recover what was lost in the garden. He comes to reconcile humanity's relationship with God, restore human relationships, and create a movement of peace in the world.

Jesus shows a broken world the image of the invisible God. Jesus shows everyone through his life and teachings how to restore the peace of God. He embodies on the cross, in his self-emptying death, the very things he taught during his life. Jesus proclaims good news for the widow, the orphan, the poor, and those from the margins of society (Luke 4:14-30). Jesus even offers peace to his enemies, to those who oppress, marginalize, and discredit him. Perhaps most scandalously, Jesus calls all his followers to do the same.

Through Jesus' blood shed on the cross (Colossians 1:19) and resurrection, God set about reconciling all things back to himself (2 Corinthians 5:19). This is the ultimate means of bringing justice, of setting all things right. This is why Isaiah's and Micah's prophecies are said to be fulfilled in Jesus, who "is our peace" (Ephesians 2:14; Colossians 1:20; Luke 2:14). Jesus' resurrection is the answer to sin and death (1 Corinthians 15:17; Romans 4:25; 1 Peter 1:3), and we now have the opportunity to be ambassadors of God's peace (2 Corinthians 5:19-20).

Through the power of the Spirit, followers of Jesus live in the space between the climax and consummation of peace.

Scan the QR code to watch the Session Five Myth & Material video. As you watch the video, write down any statements that stand out to you or thoughts that you have.

Myth

Jesus only cares about our personal salvation and personal holiness.

Material

To be a disciple of Jesus means we must learn his way of making peace in this world.

DISCUSSION QUESTIONS

01 Have you ever heard or been told that followers of Jesus shouldn't focus on justice?

02 What are ways that Christians (and by extension the American church) refuse to challenge the status quo today?

03 In what ways did Jesus disrupt cycles of violence, oppression, and injustice?

04 How can you join Jesus in his holistic ministry of reconciliation today?

Benediction

May you be blessed to receive the good news that, through Christ, you have peace with God.

May the Spirit cause this good news to be a balm for your wounds, to lift up your head, and to flood your soul with hope.

May you know that your reconciliation with God is not the end, but the beginning of a new life in which the reconciliation of all things is the end for which you live.

And may you, with the strength and courage of God, take up your cross and embody the self-giving love of Jesus for the sake of our world.

Amen.

Go in Peace.

Motion

Visio Divina

_ a guide by spiritual director
Osheta Moore

The practice of *Visio Divina* (Latin for *divine seeing*) is a prayer practice that creates space to listen and pay attention to God in our lives. Based on the monastic practice of *Lectio Divina*, where the object of prayer is a passage of Scripture, Visio Divina allows the Spirit to speak to us through images.

Center Down: All of our Motion pieces invite us to embody our practices, so find a comfortable position and gaze at the picture on the next page. Breathe slowly and intentionally while gazing at it. Ask the Spirit to illuminate something specific you see in the picture: a color, an expression, anything.

Is there a place in the image where your eyes linger or that invokes a strong reaction? Pay attention to that. Don't overthink it or explain it away. There's something in that detail for you. Where do you experience resistance in the picture? Pay attention to any uncomfortable emotions you feel while looking at the image.

Pray: "Lord, help me be a sacrificial peacemaker like you."

Take a second, longer look.

Respond: What is the invitation in this moment of your life? In the day-to-day life you are living, what is God calling you to do or be? What insights have you gained? What invitation is growing in you? What work would you like to do today? Journal your reaction to the picture.

Gratitude: Thank God for the artist and this moment. Then take a few moments of stillness in this space.

SESSION SIX

The Consummation of Peace

The Co mation

Establishment
Disruption
Call
Climax
Consummation

nsum-
of Peace

This week is about the finale of the story.
This week is about heaven meeting earth.
It is about all things being set right.

Last week we learned about the climax of the story of peace in the life and ministry of Jesus. In this session, we learn about how the story of God comes to its climactic end. We study where the world is headed and how the restoration of all things will play out in the here and the now. Where is creation headed? How do we imagine the world into the future?

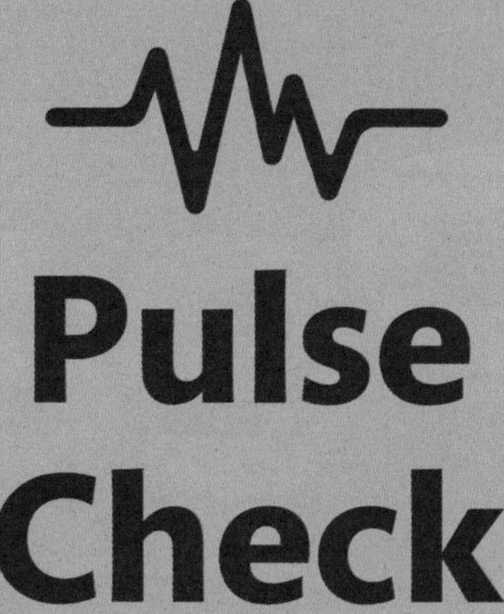

Pulse Check

Last week you spent time gazing at the love of Jesus through Visio Divina.

Before you begin Session Six spend time sharing how Jesus' love as depicted in the art at the end of Session Five makes you feel about your identity as Beloved and your calling to be a peacemaker.

Preparation

To prepare for Session Six, follow the grounding practice and read the accompanying prayer. Be present with those you are with, and be attentive to what God might impress on you during this time.

We start with a grounding practice because the world we live in is always on the go. We're often expected to show up, produce, and execute. This is a time for us to come together and consider shalom—God's dream for us to be whole, flourishing, and at peace. Shalom is God's dream for us to be fully human. This grounding practice reminds you to slow down, breathe, and invite the God of Peace to settle you before you begin with the group study.

GROUNDING PRACTICE

Take three Deep Breaths

Inhale: God of Peace
Exhale: I am Here

Inhale: God of Peace
Exhale: I am Yours

Inhale: God of Peace
Exhale: I am Ready

A Prayer on Shalom
– Based on the Psalter

O Dios,

We praise you because you are our deliverer and defender, the One who exalts the lowly and remembers his people.

O GOD, let us not return oppression with oppression. Let us not speak peace with our mouths while our hands and our hearts pursue evil. Equip us as your body to together pursue your peace with boldness, peace that is not naive but sacrificially mirrors your steadfast justice and love. Help us to know that even when you seem silent, you are still working. Help us to participate in this work.

En el nombre de Jesús te pedimos,

Amen.[1]

Manifesto

King Jesus returns to renew all things, including peace and justice, once and for all.

Revelation 21:3-8, 21-27

And I heard a loud voice from the throne saying,
"See, the home of God is among mortals.
He will dwell with them;
they will be his peoples,
and God himself will be with them and be their God;
he will wipe every tear from their eyes.
Death will be no more;
mourning and crying and pain will be no more,
for the first things have passed away."
And the one who was seated on the throne said, "See, I am making all things new." Also he said, "Write this, for these words are trustworthy and true." Then he said to me, "It is done! I am the Alpha and the Omega, the Beginning and the End. To the thirsty I will give water as a gift from the spring of the water of life. Those who conquer will inherit these things, and I will be their God, and they will be my children. But as for the cowardly, the faithless, the polluted, the murderers, the sexually immoral, the sorcerers, the idolaters, and all liars, their place will be in the lake that burns with fire and sulfur, which is the second death." . . .
And the twelve gates are twelve pearls, each of the gates is a single pearl, and the street of the city is pure gold, transparent as glass.
I saw no temple in the city, for its temple is the Lord God the Almighty and the Lamb. And the city has no need of sun or moon to shine on it, for the glory of God is its light, and its lamp is the Lamb. The nations will walk by its light, and the kings of the earth will bring their glory into it. Its gates will never be shut by day—and there will be no night there. People will bring into it the glory and the honor of the nations. But nothing unclean will enter it, nor anyone who practices abomination or falsehood, but only those who are written in the Lamb's book of life.

In the book of Revelation, Jesus returns to earth and confronts the empires of the world. Jesus speaks of a time when those who choose to reject God will no longer be able to victimize the poor, dominate the weak, or reject the image of God (imago Dei) that resides within them. The perfection of God's creation will be made possible by the return of King Jesus to earth.

The peace that was lost in the garden and reclaimed powerfully through the life, death, and resurrection of Jesus will one day be consummated by God in Jesus' ultimate return.

We exist to live into the inevitable return of Jesus on earth and help wipe tears, confront evil, and share Jesus with a hurting world.

We exist to live in response to the birth, life, death on the cross, resurrection, and ascension of Jesus. We exist to shine light on the path forward toward joining Jesus in the restoration of all things.

Scan the QR code to watch the Session Six Myth & Material video. As you watch the video, write down any statements that stand out to you or thoughts that you have.

Myth

Peace in the world is fully and completely up to us.

Material

We engage in the work of peace because Jesus is coming back.

DISCUSSION QUESTIONS

01 Session Six discusses two myths: (1) disengaging from the world is the best path and (2) saving the world is all on you. Which one are you more prone to believing?

02 How do Paul's words in 1 Corinthians 15:58 encourage you to keep working for peace and justice?

03 In what ways can you be a person who lives in the tension of having one foot in the world that is passing away, while also glimpsing God's new world that Jesus will fully usher in one day? What are healthy and holistic ways to practice this in your life today?

Spend some time meditating on your answers from the discussion questions. Write a prayer of confession in the space below.

Benediction

May God bless you with the ability
to recognize that the world is not yours to save.

May the Spirit awaken you to the beautiful truth
that you have a part to play.

May your eyes see resurrection
in the midst of this decay.

And may you hold fast to the word
that your labor is not in vain.

Amen.

Go in Peace.

Motion

Parting Prayer

_ written by Paul Alcorn

As we depart,
Both individually and collectively
Be who you are called to be.
In any and in all the ways you can
Seek justice.
Resist evil.
Stand strong against Death.
And all Death's works and wiles.
Add your voice.
Move your feet.
Extend your hands.
And because it just might
Hold on to that long arc of history like your lives depend on it.
And pull
With as little or as much strength you have
So that together we might help it continue to bend in the direction of justice.
And peace.
And hope.
And promise.
For you and for me.
For us and for them.
For all of the children of God.
So, having been nourished by this evening's gathering
Its words and its witness.
Go now and be Peace.
Amen.

NOTES

How to Use this Study

[1]Lisa Sharon Harper, *The Very Good Gospel* (New York: Penguin Random House, 2016), 14.

Session 1: The Story of Peace

[1]Howard Thurman, "How Good to Center Down!", *Meditations of the Heart* (Boston, MA: Beacon Press, 1953), 28.

Session 2: The Establishment of Peace

[1]Broken or damaged.

[2]This prayer was written by Maggie Johnson and originally appeared in Made for PAX's digital prayer book, *Tethered: 21 Prayers of Pax for and by Gen Zers of Color.*

[3]Parker Palmer, *Let Your Life Speak* (San Francisco: Josey-Bass, 2000), 4.

Session 3: The Disruption of Peace

[1]This prayer was written by Quina Aragon and originally appeared in Made for PAX's digital prayer book, *Tethered: 21 Prayers of Pax for and by Gen Zers of Color.*

Session 4: The Call of Peace

[1]This prayer was written by Hannah Chao and originally appeared in Made for PAX's digital prayer book, *Tethered: 21 Prayers of Pax for and by Gen Zers of Color.*

Session 5: The Climax of Peace

[1]Psalm 139:13.

[2]This prayer was written by Daniela Lancara Espinoza and originally appeared in Made for PAX's digital prayer book, *Tethered: 21 Prayers of Pax for and by Gen Zers of Color.*

Session 6: The Consummation of Peace

[1]This prayer was written by Giselle Gayton and originally appeared in Made for PAX's digital prayer book, *Tethered: 21 Prayers of Pax for and by Gen Zers of Color.*

MADE FOR PAX BIBLE STUDIES

MADE FOR PAX

Mental Health
A 6-Week Interactive Bible Study
Experiencing God's Care for Our Mind, Body, and Spirit
Dorcas Cheng-Tozun

Let Peace Reign
A 6-Week Interactive Bible Study
Love, Justice, and Dignity in God's Kingdom
Drew Jackson

Migration
A 6-Week Interactive Bible Study
Experiencing God's Care for Immigrants
Alexis Busetti and Dorcas Cheng-Tozun

Liberated at the Cross
A 6-Week Interactive Bible Study
Peace and Reconciliation in God's Kingdom
Kristel Acevedo

Liberados en la cruz
Un estudio bíblico interactivo de 6 semanas
Paz y reconciliación en el reino de Dios
Kristel Acevedo

Made for PAX provides faith resources by Christians of color and empowers Christians of color through the PAX Fellowship, a nine-month program serving contemplatives, creatives, community builders, and church leaders at the intersection of peace, justice, and contemplation.

To learn more, visit ***www.madeforpax.org***.